OCEANS

First published in the UK in 2019 by

Ivy Kids

An imprint of The Quarto Group
The Old Brewery
6 Blundell Street
London N7 9BH
United Kingdom
www.QuartoKnows.com

A CIP record for this book is available from the Library of Congress.

ISBN: 978-1-78240-910-6

This book was conceived, designed & produced by

Ivy Kids

58 West Street, Brighton BN1 2RA, United Kingdom

PUBLISHER	Susan Kelly
MANAGING EDITOR	Susie Behar
ART DIRECTOR	Hanri van Wyk
DESIGNER	Kevin Knight
IN-HOUSE DESIGNER	Kate Haynes
IN-HOUSE EDITORS	Lucy Menzies &
	Hannah Dove

Manufactured in Guangdong, China TT052019

1 3 5 7 9 10 8 6 4 2

My FIRST
Fact File

OCEANS

EVERYTHING you NEED to KNOW

BY DR. JEN GREEN   ILLUSTRATED BY WESLEY ROBINS
CONSULTANT: DR. DIVA AMON

IVY KIDS

CONTENTS

EVERYTHING you NEED to KNOW

INTRODUCTION

Have you ever heard of the Blue Planet? Well, guess what ... you are living on it right now! Over two-thirds of Earth's surface is covered by water and most of this is made up of salty seas and oceans. These underwater worlds are fascinating, deep, and dramatic. Get ready to dive in and explore.

This book will take you on a voyage of discovery, from the mighty forces that shape the shore and affect our weather to the deepest, darkest depths. For centuries the oceans remained a mystery and even now there is so much left to discover. Find out how tides are linked to the moon, visit coral kingdoms, and meet the weird and wacky creatures that live in the deepest, darkest parts of the oceans. Uncover the perils of the seas, from shipwrecks to hurricanes, and read about the first ocean explorers.

The oceans play a vital role in our world today and we rely on them for food, travel, energy, and much more. But they are in danger. Learn how climate change and the actions of human beings are causing harm to our waters and find out about the things we can do to help save them.

All sorts of creatures thrive in the oceans.

THE FIVE GREAT OCEANS

Since the 15th century, ships have crossed the Atlantic.

Earth has five great oceans: the Pacific, Atlantic, Indian, Southern, and Arctic. They are all connected, which means that when you go swimming in the sea, you are bathing in water that has circulated through all of Earth's oceans and seas. Have you noticed that ocean water is salty? This is because it contains minerals that rivers have washed out to sea from land.

North America

Pacific Ocean

South America

SINK OR SWIM?

Salt increases the density of water, making it easier for objects to float. This is why it's easier to float in the sea than in fresh water. You can test this at home.

You need:
A glass
Water
An egg
Salt
A tablespoon
An adult helper

1. Fill a glass with water.
2. Place an egg gently in the water. See what happens.
3. Remove the egg. Add two tablespoons of salt and stir briskly.
4. Put the egg in again. The salt means the egg now floats.

Polar bears live in the Arctic — the coldest of all the oceans.

Clownfish swim in the warm waters of the Indian Ocean.

Arctic Ocean

Europe

Asia

Atlantic Ocean

Africa

Pacific Ocean

Indian Ocean

Australia

Southern Ocean

Penguins survive in the freezing Southern Ocean.

QUICK FACTS

Earth has five great oceans and many smaller seas.

The Pacific Ocean is the largest and deepest ocean. At its widest point, it stretches halfway around the world.

WIND AND WAVES

Ocean water is never still—it is constantly moved by waves, tides, and currents (see pages 12—13). Waves are caused by wind blowing across the surface of the water. The stronger the wind, the bigger the waves it stirs up. The highest point of a wave is called its "crest" and the lowest point in between crests is the "trough." Watching a stormy sea, you might think that the wave moves far across the oceans. In fact, it moves in a circle—that's why birds on the surface bob up and down in the same place.

Waves rear up as they approach the shore.

The back of the wave moves faster than the front. The wave becomes too high and breaks.

Out at sea, winds create ripples called waves.

MAKING WAVES

The wind and the shallower water toward the shore push the wave upward.

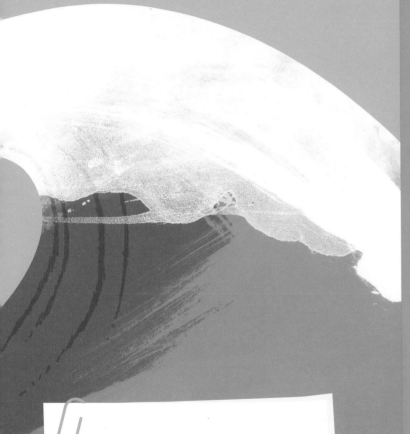

Try this experiment next time you take a bath. Or, you could fill a bowl with water.

1. Blow gently across the water's surface. Even the faintest puff produces ripples.
2. Place a plastic duck or other floating object on the surface.
3. Blow again, but not directly at the object.
4. The object will ride the waves, but it should stay in about the same place.

QUICK FACTS

Waves are made by winds blowing across the water. The waves break as they reach the shore.

CURRENTS AND TIDES

The current is the direction in which water moves. It flows like rivers through the oceans. Surface currents are caused by winds blowing across the ocean's surface. They flow in circles and help spread the sun's heat around the globe. For example, they cause warm water from the tropics to flow toward the North and South Poles. Twice a day, the sea level rises and water washes up the shore to flood beaches and then falls back again. These changes are called tides. They are caused by the moon's gravity pulling on our oceans.

MAKE A CURRENT

You need:

A bowl

Water

Talcum powder

An adult helper

1. Fill the bowl with water and sprinkle a little talcum powder on the surface.
2. Blow gently across the middle of the bowl. The talcum-covered water will flow in two circles, one turning clockwise and the other counterclockwise. Your blowing is like the strong winds that make the ocean currents.

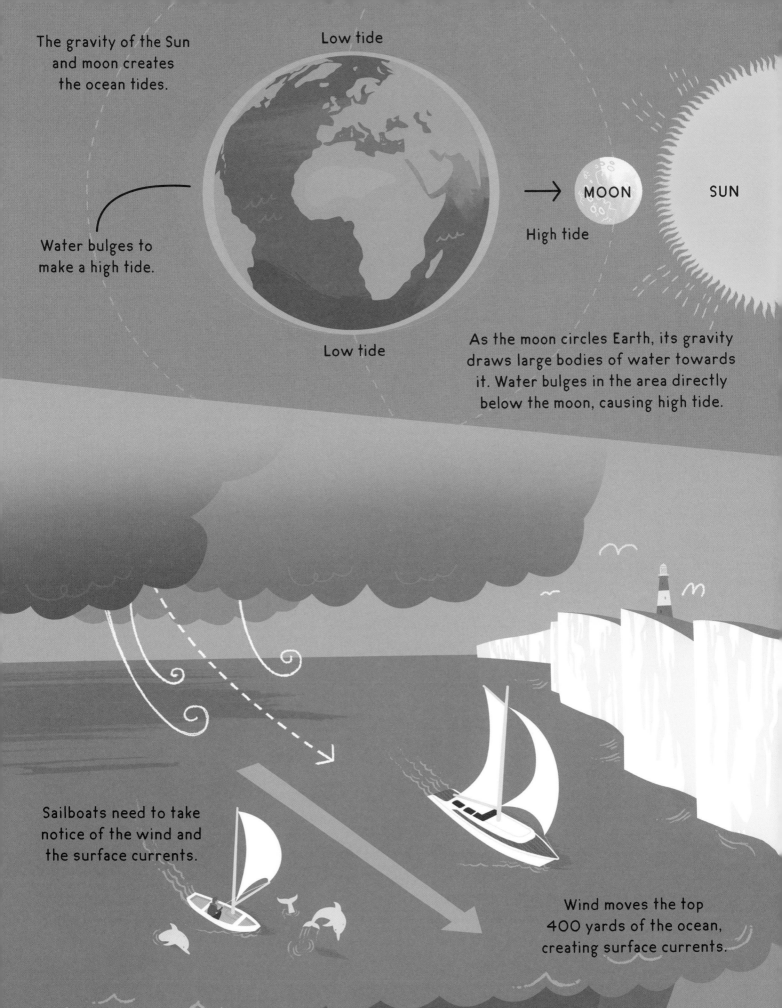

The gravity of the Sun and moon creates the ocean tides.

Low tide

MOON

SUN

High tide

Water bulges to make a high tide.

Low tide

As the moon circles Earth, its gravity draws large bodies of water towards it. Water bulges in the area directly below the moon, causing high tide.

Sailboats need to take notice of the wind and the surface currents.

Wind moves the top 400 yards of the ocean, creating surface currents.

13

OCEAN FLOOR

The ocean floor isn't flat. It has mountains and volcanoes and trenches—just as you find on land. These things are created by "plates." You could think of these as large moving slabs of rock that clash together, scrape past one another, or pull apart. When they are pulled apart, the hot rock they lie on surges up and forms volcanoes and, eventually, mountains. Two plates rubbing together can cause earthquakes.

QUICK FACTS

There are mountains, volcanoes, and deep trenches (narrow ditches) in the ocean floor created by the movement of Earth's "plates."

VOLCANIC ISLANDS

Islands are areas of land entirely surrounded by water. Some islands are made when an underwater volcano erupts on the ocean floor. Lava piles up to form an underwater peak called a "seamount." If the seamount keeps growing, it eventually breaks through the surface of the sea and becomes an island.

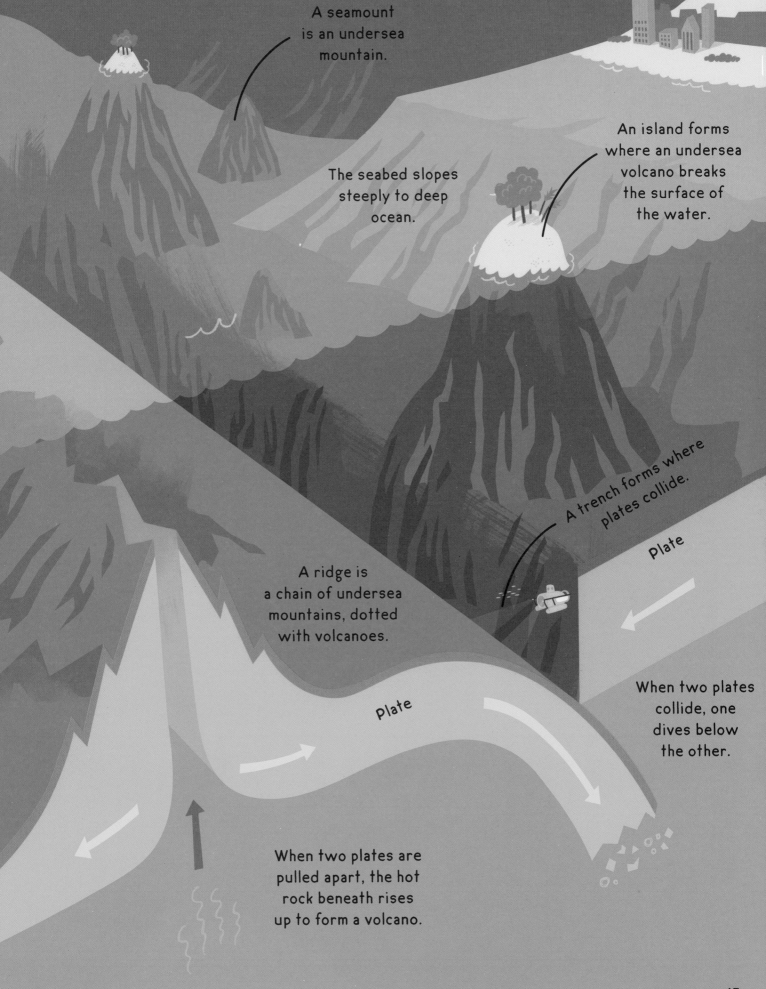

A seamount is an undersea mountain.

The seabed slopes steeply to deep ocean.

An island forms where an undersea volcano breaks the surface of the water.

A trench forms where plates collide.

A ridge is a chain of undersea mountains, dotted with volcanoes.

Plate

Plate

When two plates collide, one dives below the other.

When two plates are pulled apart, the hot rock beneath rises up to form a volcano.

SHAPING THE SHORE

Coasts are where the land meets the ocean. The wind and waves beat against the coast every minute of the day. In calm weather, this is gentle, but in stormy weather the waves crash into the land. The waves hit against the shore, acting like sandpaper and rubbing away at the land. This is called "erosion." Gradually, over many years, rocks from cliffs can fall into the sea and even clifftop houses are sometimes swept away.

QUICK FACTS

Seawater continually wears away the land. This is called erosion.

WAR OF THE WAVES

You need:

Modeling clay

A square bowl or high-sided cake pan

Sand

Water

An adult helper

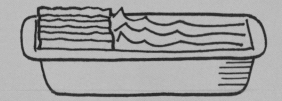

1. Mold three slabs of modeling clay about 1.5 inches high, 1 inch wide, and 2.5 inches long.
2. Lay the slabs along one end of the container or pan with the long edges jutting into the middle like headlands.
3. Pour sand between the headlands, to represent soft rocks at the coast.
4. Add water at the far end of the bowl to a depth of 1 inch. Lift the bowl to slosh the water back and forth. You'll see that the soft "rocks" wear away quickly.

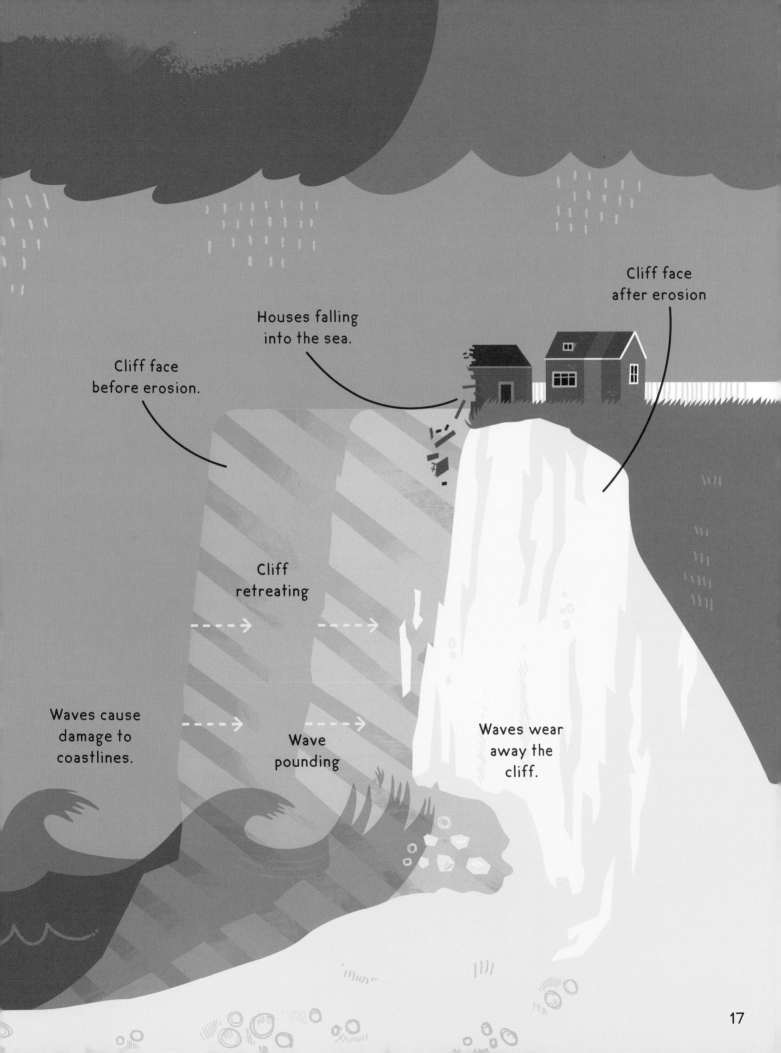

Cliff face
after erosion

Houses falling
into the sea.

Cliff face
before erosion.

Cliff
retreating

Waves cause
damage to
coastlines.

Wave
pounding

Waves wear
away the
cliff.

SUNLIT SURFACE

The Sun's rays light up and heat the surface waters.

There are different levels of the oceans from the surface to the depths, and each is home to different animals. Plants of all sizes live near the surface, where they use sunlight to make food and to grow. Many animals, from sea otters to dolphins, live here too.

Seabirds swoop down to catch fish just below the surface.

Many fish live in the sunlit surface.

QUICK FACTS

The sunlit surface waters of the oceans are full of life.

These waters are rich in oxygen and warmer than the deeper levels.

Sea otters dive for sea urchins to eat.

Kelp forests are one type of habitat lit by the Sun.

SWIM LIKE A FISH

Tiny creatures live in the warm water on the surface.

Dolphins breathe air through their blowhole.

Jellyfish use stinging tentacles to capture prey.

Kelp (a type of seaweed) contains air pockets to help it float.

Some crabs sift for food on the sea floor.

Fish, seals, and whales have smooth, streamlined bodies, shaped like torpedoes, that slip easily through the water. You can test how your body shape changes movement in a swimming pool with an adult helper. Stand in the shallow end and try to walk normally. You'll find it's impossible to do so because the water pushes against you, producing a force called drag. Now float on your stomach and swim forward. In this position your body is more streamlined, like the shape of a seal or dolphin. This reduces drag and makes it easier to move through the water.

DARK DEPTHS

Beneath the sunlit zone are deeper, darker zones. In the first, the Twilight Zone, there are glimmers of light. Below this, in the Midnight Zone and then the Abyssal Zone, there is no light at all. There is little food and no plants grow in these dark waters, but, still, some fish do live here. They have special features that allow them to survive in the cold and dark with limited food.

The stretchy stomach of the gulper eel allows it to eat prey much bigger than itself.

SHINE A LIGHT

The viperfish has huge fangs.

Some fish in the deep ocean make their own light using special chemicals. Viperfish have a row of lights on their bellies to disguise their shadows. Flashlight fish switch their little lights on and off to attract a mate. Deep-sea angler fish have a long fin with a lighted tip dangling in front of their mouths. Fish that are attracted to the light are snapped up by the giant mouth.

TWILIGHT ZONE:
650 — 3,000 FEET

Flashlight fish have pockets
under their eyes
that give off light.

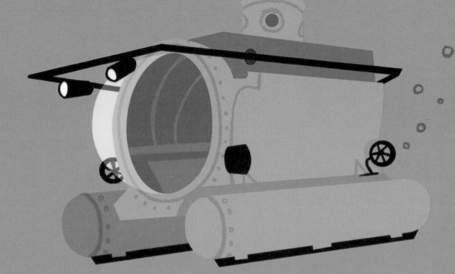

Submersibles can dive
to great depths.

MIDNIGHT ZONE:
3,300 — 13,000 FEET

The deep-sea
angler fish hunts
using a glowing
built-in fishing rod.

QUICK FACTS

There are three deep zones in
the oceans: the Twilight Zone, the
Midnight Zone, and the Abyssal
Zone. Even though they are dark
and cold, some creatures are
able to survive here.

ABYSSAL ZONE:
13,000 — 20,00 FEET

The tripod fish has
fins that direct
food toward
its mouth.

Some deep-sea creatures
give off light — this is
called bioluminescence.

"Ooze" is a sediment on the
floor of the Abyssal Zone.

FOOD CHAINS

In the oceans, the rule is eat or be eaten! Sea creatures depend on one another for food. Diagrams called food chains show what creatures eat. Almost all food chains start with plants. Tiny plants are eaten by animals that are so small they can only be seen with a microscope. These creatures are eaten by small fish, which in turn are eaten by bigger fish. At the top of the food chain, powerful predators like sharks eat the bigger fish.

Most plants in the ocean are tiny — in fact, they are microscopic but they have a big name — "phytoplankton."

QUICK FACTS

In an ocean food chain, plants are at the bottom and large predators like sharks are at the top.

Living things in the oceans depend on one another for food.

WHAT'S ON THE MENU?

Did you know the largest creatures in the ocean feed on the smallest? Great whales such as blue and humpback whales feed on plankton. So do the world's largest fish — whale sharks and basking sharks. These giant animals open their mouths wide and gulp plankton-rich water. Fringed plates hanging down inside their jaws filter out the plankton, which is then swallowed.

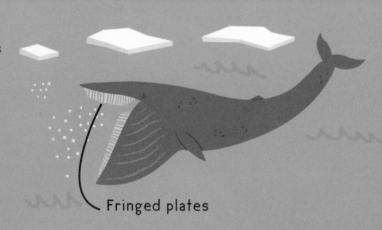

Fringed plates

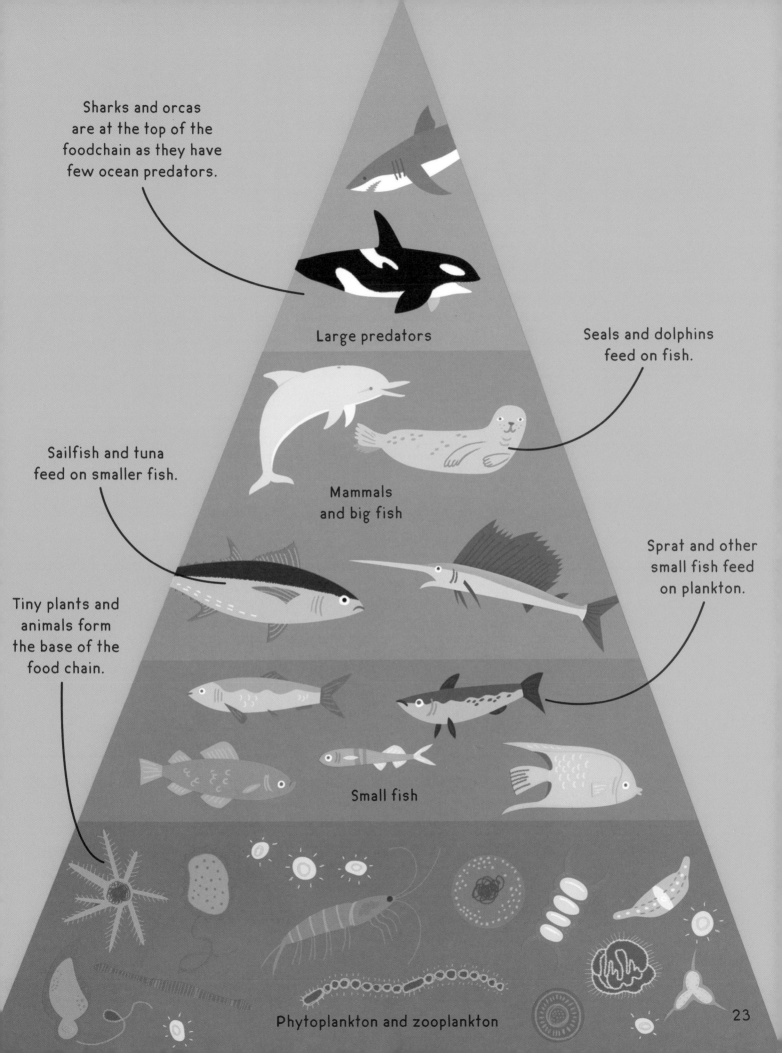

Sharks and orcas are at the top of the foodchain as they have few ocean predators.

Large predators

Seals and dolphins feed on fish.

Sailfish and tuna feed on smaller fish.

Mammals and big fish

Sprat and other small fish feed on plankton.

Tiny plants and animals form the base of the food chain.

Small fish

Phytoplankton and zooplankton

CORAL KINGDOMS

Coral reefs are found in warm, shallow seas in the tropics. Although they can be hundreds of miles long, they are made by tiny animals called coral polyps. These have soft bodies protected by skeletons. Coral reefs are like the rain forests of the sea. Teeming with life, they are home to a wide variety of sea creatures, such as brightly colored fish, giant clams, and large sea sponges.

Parrotfish bite off chunks of coral with their sharp teeth. The coral is digested and expelled as sand.

The crown-of-thorns starfish eats living coral.

THE GREAT BARRIER REEF

The Great Barrier Reef is an enormous coral reef that runs for 1,400 miles off the coast of Australia. It is thousands of years old.

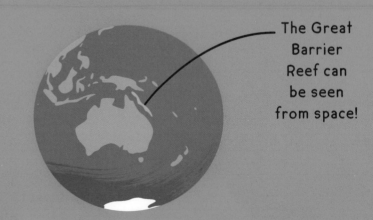

The Great Barrier Reef can be seen from space!

QUICK FACTS

Coral reefs are home to a greater variety of animals than any other ocean habitat.

Blacktip reef sharks are top predators of the reef.
Giant clams feed on plankton.
Clownfish hide among the stinging tentacles of sea anemones.
Seahorse
Polyp
The reef is formed by the chalky skeletons of coral polyps.

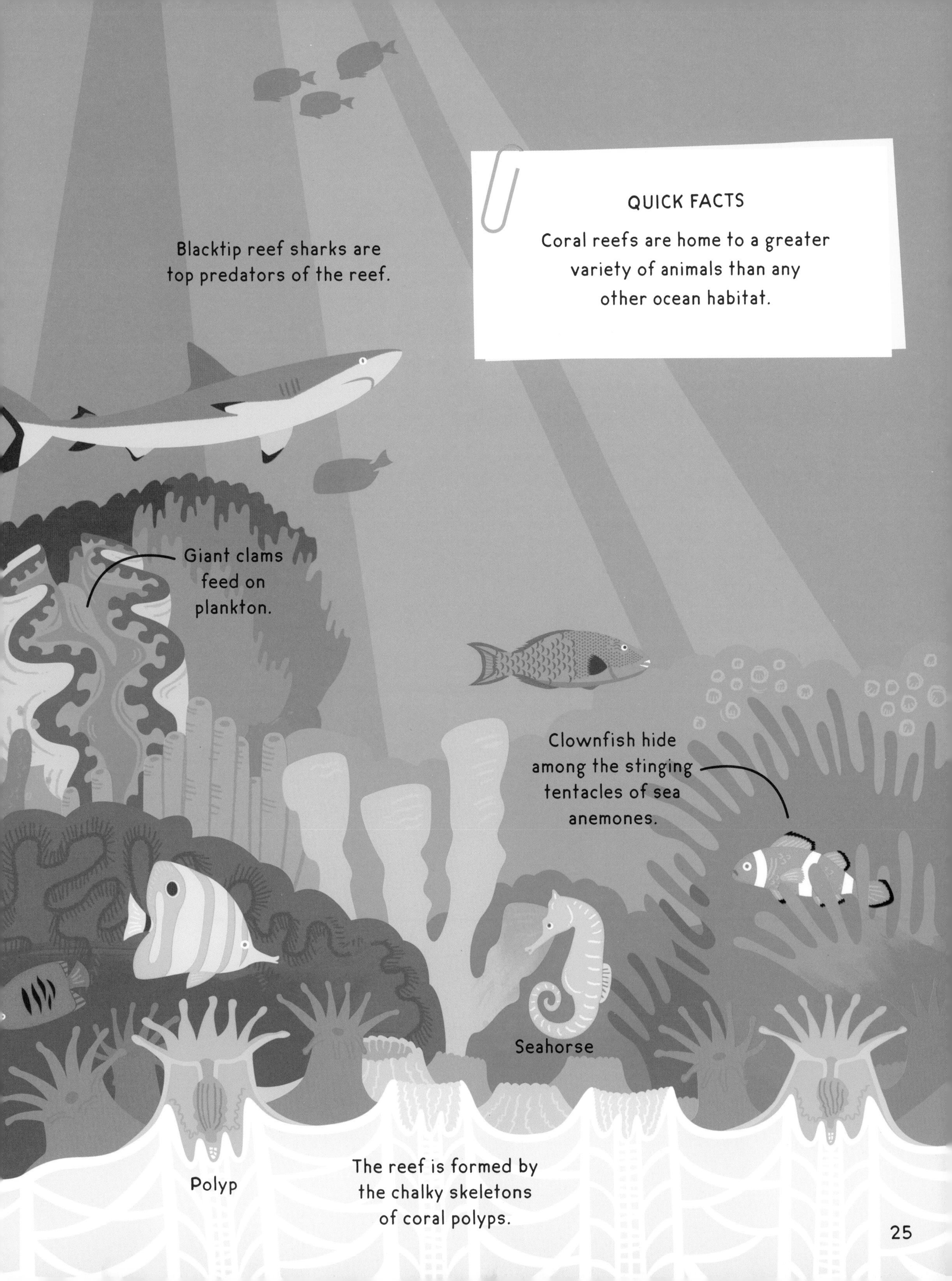

ICY HABITATS

The Arctic (including the North Pole) and Antarctic (the South Pole) are the coldest places on the planet. Very few animals live on land here, yet the seas are rich in wildlife. In spring and summer, plankton multiply on the sea surface, providing food for shrimps and krill, which in turn feed fish, whales, and other animals. Birds and mammals keep warm with thick coats of feathers or fur. Other animals, such as seals and whales, have a thick layer of fat under the skin called blubber, which protects them from the ice-cold water.

Walruses are the largest members of the seal family. They use their long tusks to pull themselves out of the water.

PENGUIN PARADISE

Antarctica is famous for penguins. Expert divers, they zoom through the water using their wings as flippers. Their greatest enemies are leopard seals, which bump into the floating ice to knock the penguins into the water.

Polar bears feed on seals, killing them when they surface to breathe.

QUICK FACTS

The Arctic and Antarctic are both extremely cold, but their seas are still rich in wildlife.

Belugas are white and blend in with blocks of ice.

Narwhals feed on fish, shrimp, and squid.

ANIMAL JOURNEYS

Not all animals spend their lives in one place in the oceans. Many use the seas as watery roads, traveling long distances to find food, escape the cold, or find a safe place to nest. These long journeys are called migrations. Imagine walking the length of a huge continent such as Africa and then, a few months later, turning around and trekking all the way back again. Many migrations are as epic as this!

Pacific salmon

The salmon hatches and grows in streams, but when it becomes an adult, it swims out to sea and lives in the open ocean.

CHAMPION MIGRATOR

The Arctic tern wins the trophy for traveling the longest distance of any migrating animal. It travels more than 44,000 miles a year, which adds up to 1.32 million miles over its 30-year lifespan. It flies from Greenland and the Arctic to Antarctica, which is from one end of the world to the other!

This globe shows the migration routes for the Pacific salmon, blue whale, and Arctic tern.

Arctic tern

- - - - - -

This tern breeds in the Arctic but flies south to feed in the Antarctic during the southern summer.

Blue whale

- - - - - -

The blue whale gives birth in warm tropical waters but migrates to the colder polar regions to feed.

QUICK FACTS

Animals such as seabirds, fish, and whales make long migrations across the oceans.

WILD WEATHER

Out at sea, huge storms called hurricanes with gale-force winds whip up rough seas with massive waves. Hurricanes are created when winds blowing from opposite directions meet and start to move upwards. In warm tropical seas, the air rises and forms huge clouds that shed rain. The winds whirl at more than 75 miles per hour. Tsunamis are massive waves, up to 50 feet high. These occur when an underwater earthquake rocks the ocean floor and causes the water above it to move violently. Waves then ripple out from this spot and race across the ocean at high speed.

QUICK FACTS

Hurricanes are huge spinning storms with whirling winds.

Tsunamis are giant waves mainly caused by underwater earthquakes.

MAKE A MINI-TSUNAMI

You need:

A bowl of water

A heavy book

A table

An adult helper

1. Fill a bowl of water and put it on the table.
2. Tap under the table below the bowl with a heavy book. The ripples that spread out are like miniature tsunamis.

Winds whirl around the "eye of the storm" (this is at the center of the hurricane).

Storm clouds shed a huge amount of rain.

The water sucked up by the hurricane forms a storm surge. This is when the storm causes the sea to rise.

Coastal towns can be flooded by the storm surge.

DANGEROUS WATERS

At sea, there are many dangers that sailors must be aware of to keep themselves safe. In shallow waters, rocks may lurk just below the surface. If ships crash into these, the rocks can rip a hole in the ship, allowing water to gush in and causing it to sink. Waves, tides, and currents can also spell danger for ships. Currents (see pages 12 – 13) can cause whirlpools, which trap and sink small boats.

Ships can crash into rocks hidden by fog.

A whirlpool (a powerful swirl of water) can trap small boats.

Loose cargo can make ships unstable.

Gale-force winds can push ships onto the shore.

Rocks just below the surface can sink ships.

RED ALERT!

Lighthouses warn sailors of dangers along the coast.

Buoys (floats anchored to the sea floor) mark dangers below the surface.

Shipwreck

There are safety measures in place to help prevent accidents at sea. Lighthouses warn of jagged rocks. Buoys mark safe lanes for ships to pass through. Radar and satellite on ships let sailors know exactly where they are in the water so they can avoid obstacles.

QUICK FACTS

There are many dangers for both ships and boats in coastal waters, including rocks and strong currents.

RISING SEAS

High in the air, gases such as carbon dioxide act like the glass in a greenhouse and trap the Sun's heat. For millions of years, this has kept the planet warm, but now pollution from cars, power stations, and cities has created more carbon dioxide, which has trapped more heat. The heat is causing ice to break off ice sheets in the Arctic and melt in the ocean. The increase of water in the ocean can cause flooding in coastal areas.

QUICK FACTS

Gases such as carbon dioxide (CO_2) trap heat from the Sun inside Earth's atmosphere and cause it to warm up.

MELTING ICE CAPS

You need:

Modeling clay

A clear plastic container

Ice cubes

A measuring jug filled with water

A marker pen

An adult helper

1. Mold a modeling clay "island" about 1.5 inches high that will comfortably fit into your plastic container.
2. Lay your "island" in the container then place 3 — 4 ice cubes on top of the island.
3. Add cold water to the container until the level is at least one-third the height of your island. Use a marker pen to mark the water level on the outside of the container.
4. Leave your "island" for a few hours or until all the ice cubes have melted. What has happened to the water level?

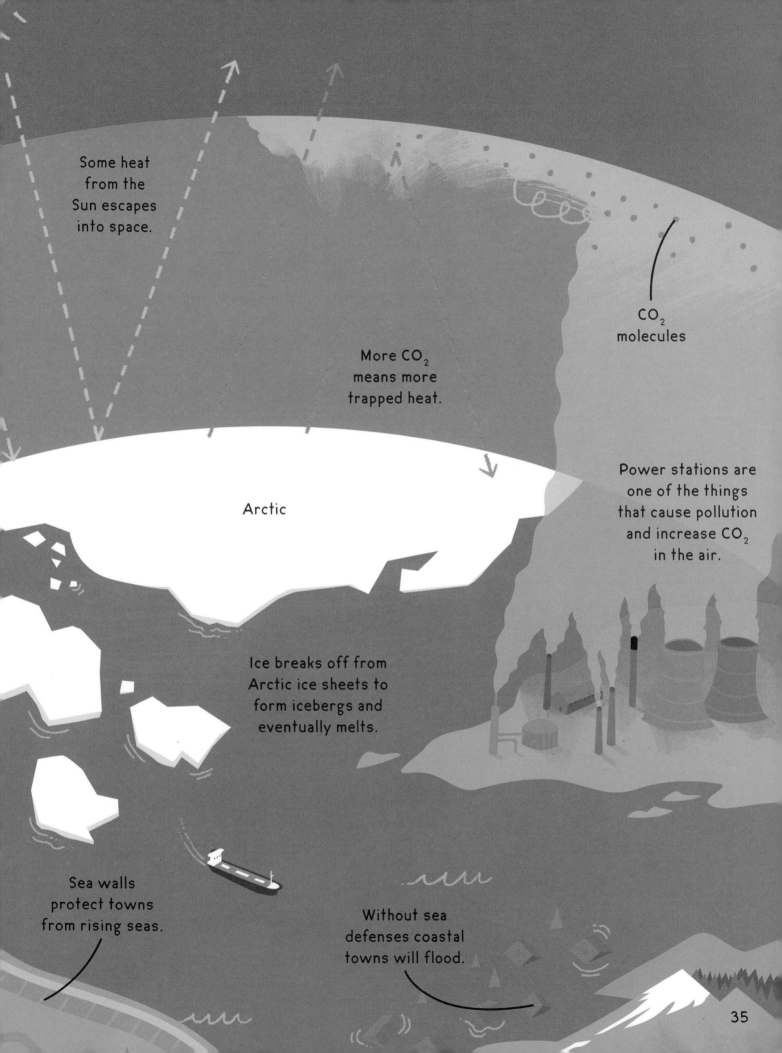

Some heat from the Sun escapes into space.

CO_2 molecules

More CO_2 means more trapped heat.

Power stations are one of the things that cause pollution and increase CO_2 in the air.

Arctic

Ice breaks off from Arctic ice sheets to form icebergs and eventually melts.

Sea walls protect towns from rising seas.

Without sea defenses coastal towns will flood.

SHIPS AND BOATS

The first boats were built about 10,000 years ago. They were simple rafts and canoes built from wood or reeds. They were mostly used for fishing and for carrying people across rivers, lakes, and around the coast. Later, sails were invented, which used wind to help power the boats. This meant sailors could travel even longer distances. Still later on steam engines were introduced, and then diesel engines. All these developments helped ships and boats travel for longer and at faster speeds.

10,000 YEARS AGO — DUGOUT
One of the earliest types of boat, a dugout was a simple canoe made out of a tree trunk.

5,000 YEARS AGO — VIKING SHIP
Known as longships, Viking ships had sails and oars.

19TH CENTURY — CLIPPER
In the 19th century, clippers were used to sail across the world. They had three masts and were very fast.

19TH CENTURY — PADDLE STEAMER
These ships were driven through
the water by paddle wheels
powered by a steam engines.

TODAY — CONTAINER SHIP
These ships are built to move large
loads of cargo across the seas and oceans.

TODAY — CRUISE SHIP
Passenger ships include ferries,
luxury cruise ships, and hydrofoils
that skim over the water on skis.

WHY HEAVY THINGS FLOAT

You need:
Modeling clay
A bowl of water

Many ships are now made of heavy
metal, which naturally sinks. Ships float
because the boat's weight is still less
than the weight of water it pushes
away. Shape also helps. A ship's hull is
filled with air. Experiment with a lump
of modeling clay. If you roll the clay
into a ball, it will sink when placed in
water. If you mold it into a boat shape
with thin sides, it should float.

QUICK FACTS

Over time, boats have
developed from small,
wooden rowing boats
to large metal ships
powered by diesel engines.

OCEAN EXPLORATION

People have always wanted to explore the oceans. They often did this without maps or compasses, and relied on the position of the Sun and stars to guide them. Ocean exploration really took off in the 15th century and a famous explorer of that time was Christopher Columbus, who sailed across the Atlantic Ocean from Spain to the Americas. At this time, sailors had to survive terrible conditions on long voyages.

Drinking water was hard to come by, so sailors drank beer and rum instead.

Food was often infested with maggots.

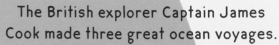
The British explorer Captain James Cook made three great ocean voyages.

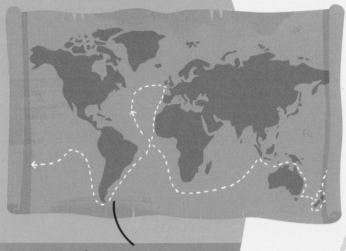

Cook's first journey took him from England across the Atlantic to the Pacific and Australia, before returning to England.

Potatoes were brought to Europe by explorers from South America.

Punishments included keel hauling, which meant a person was tied to a rope and pulled under the ship.

SHIP MATES!

Do some fun research and match the explorers (left) with their most famous ships (right). Why not challenge a friend to see who can finish it first?

Christopher Columbus	THE ENDEAVOUR
Vasco da Gama	THE SANTA MARIA
Ferdinand Magellan	THE TRINIDAD
Henry Hudson	THE DISCOVERY
James Cook	THE SAO GABRIEL

QUICK FACTS

In the 15th and 16th centuries, explorers took to the sea looking for new lands. They faced danger and horrible conditions.

EXPLORING UNDERWATER

Underwater exploration began in the 1700s, when diving suits were invented. Divers breathed air pumped from the surface through a tube, and they weren't able to move around freely. In the 1940s, the aqualung was invented. Divers could now strap tanks of compressed air to their backs and move around freely. To explore deep in the oceans, divers use small submarines called submersibles.

Scuba divers can reach depths of about 130 feet.

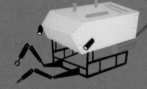

Manned and unmanned submersibles can reach depths of 6,500 feet.

In 1960, a submersible reached Earth's deepest point (below 35,797 feet).

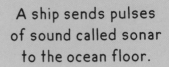

A ship sends pulses of sound called sonar to the ocean floor.

DIVING FOR TREASURE

Sonar measures the timing of the echoes it picks up.

In some parts of the oceans, fabulous treasure such as gold, silver, and pearls lies on the seabed. Most of this has come from old shipwrecks. Marine archeologists and salvage experts find sunken treasure and bring it to the surface. In deeper water, crafts called submersibles go underwater to locate wrecks.

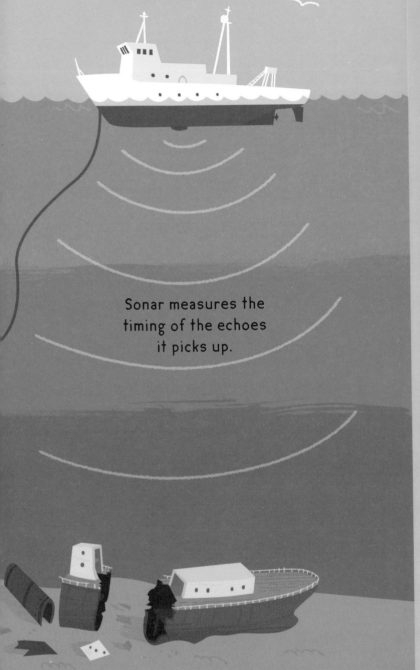

Shipwrecks can be found using sonar.

QUICK FACTS

Technology has allowed people to explore deeper and deeper parts of the oceans.

RICHES FROM THE SEA

Since ancient times, animals and plants in the seas and oceans have provided food for people. Everything from fish, shrimps, crabs, and lobsters to seaweed can be eaten. But the oceans hold many natural treasures besides food. Minerals such as gold and diamonds are found, as well as fuels such as oils and natural gas. And today, we have tidal stations that harness the energy of the tides to make electricity.

We drill for oil beneath the ocean floor.

Wave farms at sea turn wind into energy.

OVERFISHING

Every year, 100 million tons of fish are taken from the seas and oceans. Many species of fish have become scarce. This problem is called overfishing. Creatures such as dolphins, seals, and turtles also die in fishing nets.

Plastic found in everyday items, such as a car's headlights, is made from oil from the ocean.

QUICK FACTS

The oceans provide a variety of food, from fish and shellfish to seaweed. They also provide useful minerals, fuels, and energy.

Here is just some of the seafood we can get from the ocean.

Herring

Crab

Shrimp

Mussels

Lobster

Oyster

Mackerel

Clams

Salmon

OCEAN POLLUTION

For hundreds of years, people thought that the oceans were so huge, it didn't matter if we littered them with trash. We now know that dangerous waste in the water is taken into small sea creatures and carried up the food chain (see pages 22 – 23). Poisons from our waste build up in animals such as dolphins and fish such as tuna. People in turn eat the tuna. Waste also harms coral reefs, where many sea creatures live (see pages 24 – 25).

QUICK FACTS

As there are more and more people on the planet, unfortunately there is more and more pollution in the oceans. This can harm ocean animals and plants.

LITTER

The litter that we drop can end up in the sea, where it may wash ashore on beaches. Plastic, glass, metal, and old fishing nets end up on remote islands, where they can choke or trap young birds, seals, and turtles. Out in the open ocean, there are floating "islands" of plastic litter that drift with currents and tides.

Oil spilled by tankers spreads over the ocean surface.

Cities on the coast can can create pollution.

Dolphins are poisoned by polluted fish.

Pesticides from farms wash into the sea.

Marine animals are killed by the oil.

Sea animals can get trapped in the litter we throw away.

Litter dumped at sea washes onto beaches.

Toxic waste from industries flows into the sea from rivers.

PROTECTING THE OCEANS

Conservation is about protecting resources. Today, many people are trying to protect the oceans. The oceans affect the whole planet, so anything we can do to help them will make the planet a cleaner, healthier place. Governments help by doing things like banning the dumping of waste into the oceans and setting up areas called "reserves" where no fishing can take place. People can do things, too, like not littering, using less energy, and avoiding single-use plastic — all these things can help.

Bans on whaling can protect rare species.

Beach clean-ups remove litter that can harm animals.

SAVE OUR SEAS

Marine reserves protect habitats such as coral reefs.

We can help to protect the oceans. Here are some ideas:

Join with some friends to raise money for an eco-project.

Use less energy. Turn out the lights and computers when you're not using them.

Reuse as many items at home as possible. Plastic bottles, cardboard, and scrap paper are great for craft activities.

Governments, conservation organizations, and ordinary people can all help to protect the oceans.

QUICK FACTS

Oceans are important to the whole planet, so we need to keep them clean and free from pollutants such as plastic.

GLOSSARY

CARBON DIOXIDE (CO_2) A gas breathed out by people and animals and also produced by burning carbon.

CONSERVATION Protecting things found in nature such as wildlife, and keeping the environment clean.

DENSITY The measure of how compact an item is.

GRAVITY The force that pulls objects toward the ground.

HABITAT A place where an animal lives.

HEADLAND An area of high land that sticks out from the coast into the sea

MARINE ARCHEOLOGIST A person who studies how people interact with the seas and oceans.

MINERAL A natural substance not formed from animal or plant matter, for example, gold.

PESTICIDE A substance used for killing insects or other organisms harmful to crops or animals.

PHYTOPLANKTON Tiny plant life forms in the ocean.

POLES The two points at the opposite ends of Earth, known as the North Pole and the South Pole.

POLLUTION Harmful substances that are added to land, air, or water.

PREDATOR An animal that kills other animals for food.

SEDIMENT Matter, such as rocks or sand, that settles at the bottom of a body of water.

SUBMERSIBLE A small vehicle designed to operate underwater.

TROPICS The area just above and below the Equator. The climate is warm or hot, and moist all year round.

VOYAGES Journeys taken across the ocean.

WHIRLPOOL Water moving quickly in a circular motion, produced by the meeting of opposing currents and often causing a downward spiralling action.

ZOOPLANKTON Tiny animal life forms in the ocean.